used to the dark

VICKY EDMONDS

*"...I want to unfold.
I don't want to stay folded anywhere,
because where I am folded, there I am a lie..."*

-Rainer Maria Rilke

To Lucas and Ean

Cover Design: Vicky Edmonds,
Philip C. Brautigam & Greg Theobald

Cover Photograph:
(and patience above and beyond the call of duty)
Philip C. Brautigam, Seattle, WA

ISBN 0-9639918-1-7
Library of Congress Catalog Card Number:
94-70248

First Edition 1991
Second Edition 1994

 printed on recycled text paper

published by

e) all of the above

4742 • 42nd Avenue SW, Suite 607, Seattle, WA 98116
(206) 937-0700 • (206) 763-6702
fax (206) 763-7627

WITH GRATITUDE...

*To Shelley Tucker
for creating the "Write from the Source" classes
and for her ongoing support of my work
which continues to help me every day,
to Oprah Winfrey
for her "Year of the Child" series
and her open dedication to speaking out about abuse
which has inspired many of these poems,
to Ken Verver for believing in me
all the days of writing this book,
to John Bradshaw, Terry Kellogg and
Alice Miller for their work,
to Gillian Marrah, Delphine Bowers
and Al Chase for theirs,
and presently to
Oonagh Perdue
Paul Gilman
Lori Gist
Greg Theobald
and all of the friends
too numerous to mention
for being with me
as I go.*

CONTENTS

Author's note

The writings presented in this book are about remembering what went on in my childhood, and how those seeds, once planted, grew out in my life as an adult. They are the memories, feelings and observations about the truth as I see it. Some of them aren't even clear memories, just pieces of pictures that move through my mind where they scattered after being torn up.

I do not expect that this is the same truth my mother sees, or my sister, or any neighbor that happened to glance at us from time to time, but it is mine.

FOREWORD

Many of us studied only certain types of poetry in school. These poems rhymed and dealt with unemotional themes, or they were so difficult to understand that they seemed like puzzles needing to be solved. We are so grateful, then, when we read Vicky's work because she writes poetry for healing. Her poems are significant and understandable.

Vicky shows us that subconscious thought and poetry exist in the same arena. Both give voice to memories and draw on sensory experience. Her poems especially engage our sense of sight. She is a master photographer creating series of images on paper, and her camera's main mechanism is the metaphor, a comparison between different things.

In the poem, "Cutting Room Floor", Vicky compares her mind to a tape recorder. She rewinds the tape of the past, fully remembers, and records the details. This frees her from running old messages in a continuous loop through her mind or accidentally pouring them out on her children. By writing, she externalizes these memories to examine, resolve, and heal them. She tells the truth, and, as we read her poems, we are encouraged to remember the words spoken in our houses when we were children, words we've tried to forget but notice, nonetheless, lingering in the backs of our minds or slipping out of our mouths unexpectedly.

Most of us, like Vicky, grew up with experiences that seemed unnameable. As a result, many of us have doubted the validity of our memories. By naming her experiences, Vicky claims her perceptions and her past. She gives herself and us permission to break down the walls used to compartmentalize difficult experiences, and, in doing so, we understand and integrate these into our lives.

At first, Vicky's title, ***used to the dark***, may seem bleak, but, on closer inspection, we see that the dark can only be named when one realizes that there is light. Perhaps the most difficult thing to do is what Vicky has already accomplished- turn on the spotlight and point it into those darkest corners. Once the light is shed, the truth is so compelling that it requires a closer look. Sometimes, the views she paints in her poetry are raw and explicit, but, other times, those old skeletons held up to the light actually seem funny. In "Action" and "Go To Pot", Vicky shows us how healing occurs through humor, too.

Unfocused memories are very difficult to heal. By pinpointing and naming her perceptions, Vicky goes below emotional depression and discontent to the real underlying feelings. As we read her poems, we, too, are encouraged to experience our full range of emotions. Her honesty invites us to laugh, cry, yell, rage, and smile. We have our feelings, and we heal, too.

Many of us have tried to live in the light by ignoring the dark or attempting to forget the difficult times, but we have found these strategies don't work. We still have unexplainable fears, get depressed or angry without knowing why, or feel out of control. Vicky's poetry shows a clear path for healing. By diving into the dark, she remembers and names the past, and, in reading her poetry, suddenly, we can see in the dark, too.

Shelley Tucker
Author of ***Writing Poetry***

used to the dark

I ASKED

I asked my eyes,
what did you see?
They closed
to look inside.

I asked my ears,
What are you listening for?
But they had no lips
to whisper.

I asked my feet,
How far have you come?
They sat in silence,
resting.

I asked my mind,
Can I help you find your way?
It replied,
"I haven't been lost."

WHO AM I

Who am I?
I am the dream
of waking
from the nightmare.
I am the humming
of life in limbs
that were deeply asleep.
I am the light
that catches
in your eye
when you see yourself
as worthy.
Secret gardens grow
inside you,
even though
never tended.
The rose
of your mind blooms,
but you never bring it
to your table.
Who do I think I am?
I am the daughter
mother of hope.
I am the memory of love
that you had
good reason to hate.
I am the piece of yourself
that you left
to make peace
with herself.

Used to the Dark

The dark
hurts my eyes,
straining to see
what may never come clear.
The black void
vacuums the light
and there's nothing left
but lies.
The corners of my mind
close in,
crumple and crease
to conceal what's inside,
my memory being
the smallest grey dot
at the end of a sentence
at the innermost fold.
The end of a sentence
I served to you
on the platter
of my youth.
Eight years to life
in the black of a night
where my eyes
got used to the dark.

ALLEYS

Sunken men haunt
the back alleys of my mind.
Leering and lurking
they peer up my thighs
through the spaces
in the slatted fence.
The gate swings open
in the chill of dusk,
a warning to
vulnerable
young girls in the dark.
Their eyes
follow me faster,
expecting with a smile
the place I'll put
my next fleeing foot,
but I can't run.
Like wolves that taste fear
they'd prey,
excitement of the chase
whetting their appetites.
Through the door
and locked tightly in
I can still feel their breath
coming closer,
its steamy sweat
running in my ears.
Nowhere to hide.
Locks are broken
by thieves every night
with stronger wills
than mine.

With what stick
can I beat them back?
If I make it through
tonight, tomorrow
I'll put one on
the shopping list,
the list a tablet long
of how I'll live
in a street full of alleys.

THE SCULPTURE

I think if I let you,
your breath could melt
the sculpture
of my ice.
Your wanting
warms the winds,
but I'm frozen in time
at a little past nine.
At your touch I feel
you're trying to steal
something from me
thieves already took,
and I guard the empty box
with hands and locks.
Some shallow shadow
inside cries still
at your absence,
as I turn
to the cold of stone
under years of snow.
My slick, sleek glaze
turns a stiff shoulder
to slide out
from your palm,
but your print is left there,
even though
you are gone.

ONIONS

Those onions on the counter
have gone bad,
like I used to be.
The layers lay together,
transparent,
and settle into sleep.
Once they were harsh
and strong with silent tears
still hidden deep,
but now they've gone soft
in the middle,
their shells cracked
like parchment
after years in the sun.
There's something new
appearing, though,
like a phoenix
from the fire.
Long green fingers
reaching forth to grab at life.
Coming out at the end
from its beginnings,
deep inside, and coming
through the door
as it closes
behind.

NEARER TO THE WELL

I stem from stern
uncertain soil,
parched white
in the bone dry stares
of misunderstanding.
As I uncoil
I crack the crust
and shatter the sediment
and sentiment left
on the bottom of the floor
long after the ocean is gone.
One strong spirit
still grows green
and fills the unfolding
arms of life's
long reaching
for itself.
But rooted still
in cemented past
I cast
at least my shadow
toward the spring,
and bloom and blossom
and go to seed
and catch the flight
that freedom brings
and watch my children grow
still nearer to the well.

FOR EAN

I think I could have
slept with you,
kept you in my bed
for years, if it wasn't
for what other people
might think.
Society pulls us apart
at the start
without ever saying a word,
tearing love and life
from limb to live
in distance from ourselves.
The smell of you,
the balm of your breath
warming the cool
of my sheets,
filling the space
in my arms, and
healing
the illness of age.
I long to draw you in,
but watch you safe
from behind the bars,
the aesthetic wall of distance
between mother
and son.

Window

The written word is a window,
an entrance into half hidden truths
partially covered in sheets of paper
drawn down to the middle of the pane.
Look past the blind of empty lines
to the openings between.
Unlatch the lock and let the weight
take you up inside the casings,
then follow the strings
to see how the workings work.
Pull up the glass and go through,
there is a frame to hold you safe
away from all sharp edges at your side.
No cause or need to cut or bleed,
the window opens wide,
and the curtain falls
only after you've come and gone.

She Is Me

It's easy to point the finger
at what I used to be,
talk easily about how far I've come,
until I see she's with me
hiding just behind my back
stabbing nails into my hands
to see if I'm human or a saint,
so godly now that maybe
my heart won't bleed for her.
She creeps along the shadows
and peers at every scrap of light
with eyes that pierce the night
like scalpels slicing every sight.
Shame hangs on her
like a vest of metal mesh
that she links a little longer
every day. The weight is more
when she is less
and can barely lift it up,
but she drags herself
behind me while I rest.
She is hungry, she is tired,
she will sneak and cheat and lie
and lie down with dogs
to share a bit of meat,
then she will cut them
with her claws
among the sheets.
She is angry, she is sad,
she will kill if she goes mad,
she will cut her hand off
if she can't get free.
She is me.

SHE SEES ME

for Gillian

In the silence
she hears me,
wordless whispers,
soundless scars.
In the darkness
she sees me,
hiding haunted
lost little girl.

The piece inside
that once was me
feels her perfect pitch
like a tuning fork
laid along
a bare bone,
the sound so clear
I can touch it
smoothly
with small child's
curious fingers.

In my nightmare
she finds me.
My cheek softly
on her arm,
I hold gently
not to scare,
not to hurt
and make her move,
not to lose another
mother.

DIRTY PENNIES

Sometimes I can see the rooms
where I spent my childhood
like dirty pennies,
carelessly.
Better to get rid of these
on useless things
and keep the good ones
for keeps sake.
Throw away days
took years to the trash,
was there anything left
worth saving?

Sunday school

When I was six
I was kicked
out of Sunday school.
All the girls had pretty,
full slipped dresses,
clean knees
with white socks below
and ruffles rising high.
Several seconds
after I sat down,
after begging the babysitter
to let me come,
I noticed my knees.
Green jeans
with patched knees
and dirt stains
down the front.
They didn't match
the other knees
in my row,
the front row
where I rushed to sit
so I wouldn't miss a thing.
My knees
didn't belong here.
Hot, red guilt
spilled over me,
I must've
done something wrong.
"Does everyone
have their dime
for a workbook?"
No,

I don't have a dime.
"You'll need to go
and get your dime
before you can work
in the workbook."
I loved workbooks,
and Jesus was in this one,
orange and white
with full color pictures
and words
that spoke of God.
My knees
stood me straight
and walked me out.
I could only see
the door
and the knob
and the carpet along the way.
My knees
never kneeled there,
or almost anywhere,
but I always make sure
I have a dime on me,
just in case.

RISK

Fear is a door
that creaks when it opens,
everything hinges on this.
This wall that before it
I couldn't go through,
this frame of reference
that shows me the place
designed for me
to enter.
I stop
and check the number
to see if it matches mine,
yes, I seem
to hold the only key.
I reserved this
sight unseen,
thinking
pleasant little getaway,
but all the signs say
under construction,
enter
at your own risk.

HE HAD A MONOPOLY

ON MY FIRST HOT PROPERTY

I wonder if my first time lover
even remembers my name,
or my face for that matter,
being just a piece in the game.
So busy battling with my brastrap
he lost track of his tongue in my mouth.
Not that there was anything inside
my community chest worth discovering,
but brastraps are the Reading Railroad
of teenage sex. Just one of those stops
you have to pull out from
in order to get past go.
Zippers are down along the homestretch
dodging hotels with high rents due
should you happen to stay too long
instead of just passing through.
And getting his underwear
only four inches down was just
that last damn utility you hit
when you know your racecar's come
to the end of the road,
because you can't roll a one
with two dice bouncing on the mirror
in the Park Place of tenth grade
hormone heaven.

Second Coming

If Jesus were alive today
he'd walk on Nike Air
instead of water,
and say 'Peace, be still'
to the sound
of the garbage barge.
Coming for seconds
wouldn't mean
he hasn't already
had his fill
of teaching a people
that seem
so unwilling to learn.
Come as little children
didn't mean
to act like a spoiled brat,
and the meek
shall inherit the earth
wasn't meant
to make homeless.
But how would he
get our attention,
televangelism was a flop,
and he couldn't go
door to door
because nobody's home.

HIS PRESENCE

I am new to god.
He slept at night
on the porch of my house
in a chair
leaned against the door,
gray with the night,
gray with age,
gray with the lack
of judgement
at the deeds
that went on
right inside.
Silent like a burglar
who took nothing
and gave little more
than his presence
and a calm
that whitewashed black.
Now I come
like a guest to his house
to introduce myself,
to smile
and feel embarrassed
at having met
somebody great,
to wait
on a chair on his porch
to be recognized.

INCEST

I caught his penis
in the back of my throat,
semen spurting
suffocating sperm,
white coagulating
bitter taste
left in my mouth,
I can't get it out.
I gag on the bile,
my body rejecting
the memory
of his madness.
My tongue tasted salt
on the sweaty skin
the stick shoved in
a full mouth tongue depressor,
pressed down
to keep me
from screaming out.
The veins bulged
on the sides,
the size pulsing
as he wriggled inside.
I thought I would die.
I thought I would like to.
I thought I already had.
Where does this memory
come
from,
child's imagination,
Freudian slip?
He slipped himself inside me
like a knife

and cut out the possibility
of my husband's
full love life.
Maybe he didn't put it there,
but there it is
just the same,
strangling the woman
who lives inside.

Don't talk with your mouth full,
(let's keep this just between us).

No problem,
no one comes close,
my lips are sealed.

Roots

Rage is a hatchet
pulled from my groin.
I hurl it at my enemy,
the deadly tree,
and hack away its roots,
dry and twisted skeletons
of strangled innocents.
I chop and cleave
at stubs of fingers
left clutching up at me
from below...

Then bury my axe
in the dirt
to forgive my sins.

RAW

Raw,
like fruit
left on the vine,
raw and rancid and rotting.
Like the first ripped
edges of a tree
as it's torn into two by fours.
Raw as an open cut
looked into
as it stops itself from bleeding,
solid to liquid and back
before your eyes.
Raw is the sound
of the open mouth
with something spoiled inside.
Raw is the color of red
and black and blue
under strong new light.
My hands are raw
from writing
like a buzzsaw across
the page,
my arm from letting go
the rooted rage.
Raw are my eyes
that see through panes of glass
into broken light.
Raw is the healing way
of opening wide.

TECHNICAL DIFFICULTIES

The cold comes in
like snow to my head,
like a TV that's off the air.
I'm on, but the pictures
aren't there,
just static and hum.
Not even the Indian came
in his circle of
black and white and grey
to tell me it's time to retire
at the end of the day.
I just keep looking,
wondering
if technical difficulties
will pass,
and am hypnotized
by the white
unyielding buzz
inside my brain.

Breathe easy

Breathe easy.
Now seven years
past the freezing point,
my nostrils still numb
from inches of powder
shushing down
the slope of my neck
and coming to rest
in my chest.
The snow queen
all dressed in white
with crystallized eyes
the blue of ice
and the cold
of indifferent suicide.
Ice that cuts
and melts on mirrors,
sheets of glass
that smashed into shards
slicing my reflection
into splinters
of a self,
and seven years of luck
to change my mind
and breathe in life.

Now that i know

Now that I know the place
where breath meets earth
and my ears are warmed
by the ache of having God
slip through
and into my fingers,
I can think of nothing else.
No goal rises higher
or has more than a single
dimension.

Now that I know the place
where lust meets love
with innocent touchings
watched with children's eyes
in full grown bodies,
I can settle for nothing less.

Now that I know the place
where sun shines
through drying grass
close to my ears and
arms reach around the earth
to pull it inside,
eyes closed,
and feel it's gentle turning
as I evolve,
I know there is no closer place
that I can be
to the me that is we.

THE SIZE OF THE CUP

Some people see
optimism or pessimism
in the amount of fluid in
the glass. I saw importance
in the size of the cup. Young
boy bodied with only ribs tick-
ling the smoothness of my lines,
I padded the truth a time or two to
improve my presentation. Training
bras were put on, but my chest didn't
learn a thing. My mother with a 50-Z
could easily fling one over her shoulder
and out of the way while she ate her
evening meal. And my sister who was
fully filled out by the ripe old age of
twelve, became a hot comodity by the
sixth grade. I sat by on the play-
ground and learned about supply
and demand, grateful now to be
the one in the family who
got good business sense.

TEMPORARY INSANITY

How sick do you have to be
before they consider you
mentally ill?
A little under the weather
wouldn't do.
A cold might keep you
shut in, and a flu
might force you
to feed your fever,
but delusion
would definitely kink
your thinking straight.
A migraine could cause
clear seeing to cease,
and a spasm
might force your hand
to strike out at others
accidentally
along the way.
But cancer is hard to detect,
it changes form
and attacks on site, though
a person looks perfectly fine
for quite some time.
And without diagnosis
no one would know
the disease you hide inside
is spreading to all the edges
of your mind.

LONG ARM

My father was the long arm of the law
and the longer arm of the army,
we were only privates
at the core.
He could reach us
anywhere we were
waiting for our orders.
I can still feel his hand inside me,
a puppet,
fingers moving my head
and mouth,
grip on my middle
where my stomach still clenches
against it.
One man's army,
little toy soldiers
with shoulders to carry his load.
Marionettes
with strings attached
to dance
while he took his leave.
His hand still has hold of my hair
from the grave
where he lays resisting sleep,
but I have the scissors
to cut him away from me.
He had the law on his side
as he carried out
his secret plans,
and he won all the battles,
but I will win the war.

THIEF IN THE NIGHT

I will not spill
my blood on the blade
of your knife while you hide
in my mind.
You will not pierce
my years of safety
while I lie asleep in my bed.
I take my power from you,
the thief in the night
and sieze the day,
a new light
to right your wrongs,
to write your wrongs
and be on my way.

Interlude

Stone sings
a single song,
a steely sound
from below the ground.
A round that starts
and ends with itself
but includes all others
in kind.
A small sonata,
sacred and still,
low and shrill,
a silver straw
that pierces
the silent night.
Stone sings.

LACK OF EDUCATION

I wear my lack of education
like a beautiful old wool coat
with several small holes
in the lapel
where a pin should be.
The flaws are often apparent
to silent stares,
hand sewn hem,
lack of lining, the button
missing at the top.
I obviously didn't purchase this
from some fine established shop
or ladies ready-to-wear in
lovely Cambridge, Massachusettes
where one wears one's clothing
like initials after your name
so people can see at first glance
your position in society
among those who have
and those who have not,
and those who ask,
"have what?"

BROKEN GLASS

Broken glass,
at last
when taken
one single shard
at a time,
is simply
a piece of the all
in the palm of your hand.
Look closer.
Individually inspected
you see
sharp departures
from the edge,
the hole in the whole,
the presence
of absence.
It cannot hurt you,
but you may use it
to hurt yourself.
You can walk over
broken glass.
Lay it out,
one slice at a time
with stepping space
in between,
then sweep the walk
to gather your life
behind you.

ANGUISH

She rolls in seeping swollen tears
from red soaked eyes,
glassy in the daylight.
Her face is beige
but she's leaking black
like a mud puddled tire
from inside the white walls,
like an oil spill
from a forgotten tanker,
docked on an abandoned pier,
like india ink on a wet page
from the fountain of the pen.
Sometimes I'd like to poke her with it,
make the hole larger
and let it drain out,
but she keeps it in like a separate life
that needs her shell to go on,
and I'm not sure I'd recognize her
without it. Even the smiles
show red through the teeth,
sorrow bleeding where joy should be.
She breathes it out and it peels off
the layers of skin like toxic chemicals.
It's not enough to say
clean it up, you need to
look at the damage done,
and hold her up, an example
to future generations,
a poster child
of the great depression,
an impotice
to mend our wounding ways.

LOOK FOR YOURSELF

How would we feel
good about ourselves
if there were no more
starving children
that we could give our pennies to
and then write off
at the end of the year?
If one nation's wealth
leaked into the other
like water in a circular tide,
who would we ache for
to notice we're alive?
Food enough for all the world,
clothes to keep them warm,
clean air and water
to soothe their dying shells.
If we gave until everyone
had enough
to keep themselves alive,
would we notice our own souls
wandering away in the night?
Holes is their swollen stomachs,
gaping glances in their eyes,
wordless mouths open and falling
to shadow in the black.
Say yes to the humbled,
hungry homeless,
say yes to the victims of the fire,
and then look for yourself
among the ashes.

The last time

The last time you touched me
you seemed to know who I was.
Palms on skin that had never
felt held, cheek on neck
inviting, exposing
the vulnerable parts
of my softening rigidity.
I asked you in and you came,
eyes open, hands at your side
without need of defense
or protection. You could feel
the changing of the seasons in me.
You didn't need your thick overcoat
to keep you from the cold.
Nine years of winter,
and now this gradual spring.
Bodies lingered together
without minds
spinning scary separations.
And I touched you, as if never
having known you before.
This man, this man I love.
Relaxing into the muscles
of your arms
you held lightly to me,
feeling the space between us.
Thousands of nights
we've spent together, meeting needs,
filling space, laying together
like spoons on the side.
How did we get here?
When I look in your eyes,
I usually can't find you.

You're locked into the graph
at the middle of the road,
steady as she goes,
and down so deep, so far inside,
I can barely make you out
among the shadows.
But that night, I couldn't see your eyes
in the dark of evening, with the shades
pulled down and the comforter up,
and you were there. Like a child
whose imagination goes on
just after the light goes out,
you came out without even trying.
I've never been in love with you
before. I've loved you
with good reason and sense.
The man who builds new rooms
or fixes old faucets.
A dependable man,
never straying outside the lines
of good conduct. A kind man
who cries at movies.
A strong man, gentle enough
to wrestle with babies on the floor.
But that night, you were mine.
No job in your thoughts,
no clicking inventory
in the sideways blink of your eyes.
You laid on the sheets, full bodied,
and kissed me like a boy
who really wanted to know
the taste of my lips,
and I let you.

COMING HOME TO K-MART

Whoever said that husbands
were supposed to be
the K-Mart of relationships,
your one-stop shopping
center of attention?
Sometimes he's a mall
and I still can't find
anything I want,
or even what I thought
I was looking for.
He hopes I won't go
shopping around,
and what I spend
will keep him in business,
but I'm a consumer
with a variety of needs.
He doesn't have a psychiatrist
or a dentist or tarot cards,
or slurpees
or escargot in garlic sauce.
And sometimes
he's in underwear
when I'm
in the software aisle,
or hardware or flatware
or anywhere else but there.
He's actually more
a garage sale
laid out on a table to see,
but with treasures
still hidden in dark
and cobwebbed corners.
Somebody else's old used stuff,

game pieces
that were never played,
gifts from a girl who's gone
that he doesn't want.
A hammer that still works
and a Star Trek communicator
that doesn't,
from some old future scenes
he still reruns.
But still, it's homey here
and I can feel comfortable
to browse,
and argue over the price
till I get a good deal.

THE DISTANCE

It's been my job
to keep the distance,
and I've kept it well.
I've filled the spaces
between us with space,
measured the closeness
and put you in place
at arms length
and off to the side
as you leaned into life.
I've arranged the seats
so no knees would touch,
no angles directly oppose,
supposedly to keep
peace in place
where inflated egos rose.
The rugs weren't wrinkled
to trip you up and
throw you headlong
into my arms,
the length of which
grew longer every day.
But somehow
you slid through
the electrified spaces
in my chain link life,
stepped over
the barbed wire bundles
at the end of the bed
and came inside.

Prey

He was such a beautiful boy,
it brought tears to my eyes.
All he did was cross the street
and I ached for the part of me
that had already passed.
I would never have known him,
and probably still never will.
He's gone on a journey,
a boy somewhere on his way
to becoming a man,
and I can't get directions
to that place.
On his way
to becoming someone
I'll be afraid of soon,
someday.
Where does he cross
from boy to man?
What marks the turn
between cared for
and caring for,
protected and protector,
and where does
my mind change him
into predator
from prey?

FOR STEVE

Where do you wait
for the shadows to lengthen
or shorten the passing
of your time?
Hidden around darkening corners
of backless alleys,
the stones meet your face
with the same expression.
There is no comfort here.
No color can fade
into the black
that draws you in like the night.
One piercing needle prick
can drain all the mercury
from the thermometer
of your body
and still leave the glass
intact.
Cold, useless degrees
still measure
the emptiness in your eyes.

TAKE

Take the needle from your arm.
Take up the slack
in your sagging skin
by bending
at the elbow.
Take in the breath
from your lover's exhaling,
she waits on the pillow
where you rest.
Take out the treason
with the trash
and your reasons,
let them be picked up
and gone.
Take down the wall
that hides you from yourself,
and give in to the life
that longs to meet you.

BLACK AND WHITE

We always make a good impression,
of our thumbs onto the inkpad.
White sheep with ink leaking through
till we're completely dyed in the wool.
How can I look so good to some
and still so bad to others?
I clean my closets and corners and clothes
and clearly, some work has been done.
But still next to cotton
that's never been soiled,
my stains still show their shadows.
White light, white linen,
white bread and WASPs,
but my family has always been
a hornets nest.
We sting and die by the thousands,
lie dormant
and wait for the rituals again,
without any reasoning minds
to understand.
An animal with a cloven hoof
or an insect with potential to kill,
not even Darwin could help us,
but maybe god can.

MOON

Moon listens
while the spot light looks.
Moon knows
when men are still asking.
Moon whispers
to be heard below the crowd.
Moon remembers
long after I've forgotten.

JUST THE SAME

The course of our lives
has run the same route,
but it looks very different
to you.
The banks of your stream
were lush and green
with pillaring trees
to hold the ground together.
Flowers grew on that shore.
Lovely yellow dandelions
that looked like mums
from a distance.
My bed was sharp and rocky
with jagged cliffs rising high,
slate that chipped off
with every climbing step
felling child
and deep black glistening flint
back to the current below.
No plants
to hold the earth intact
as our soil
washed down the creek.

But it was the same river
we drowned in,
just the same.

Useable parts

I uncover myself
with my words,
one small shovelful
at a time.
I unearth my body,
bare my bones,
rise my rotting flesh.
There lies
my husband's torturer,
there
my children's judge.
Like Frankenstein
I try to find
some useable parts
to put together
to make
one working whole
embodied being.
But is it monster
or child I find
that starts out
into night,
where eyes discover
rifled fright
aimed right into its heart
of hideous,
insidious sincerity.

I'll be damned

for Lucas

I strike out at you
as if you were her,
pushing my buttons
all the way to the wall
face first,
smashed against the plaster.
I gouge with fingernails
slashing deep
into the swollen underbelly
of your small child's shame.
I scream the scream
of an animal trapped in a trap,
severing its leg,
as though screaming at you
could make her hear me more.

Parents don't pass things
back up stream
to find the source
of where they came from,
they wait to break off
into tributaries
then dump their toxic waste.
New streams with foliage
tender green, budding out,
are burned beyond repair
at the first few drops,
turning rich brown soil
where something could grow
ashen and red and dead.

I see your face
in my mind at those times

like a black and white picture
of a ghost
whose eyes stare back at me
vacantly,
the mind shut down
because things won't fit,
and I see myself at five,
half dead, and waiting
for my funeral
to mark the end.

I never felt the passing of time,
just a void
where life should be.
Like a field
after an acid rain
that spills into rivers
which carry it down
and pass it on and on and on,
to you? No.
I'll be damned.

LEAVING THE PATH

The wise man sits
quietly, eyes closed.
He sees the world
and embraces
all the black and white
at once in open arms.
He has no need
to talk of his beliefs
vainly, as though
giving himself importance
above any others.
And still, many will
travel to sit at his side,
to learn to be quiet
and know his truths,
as though knowing
could save their lives.
But a healing woman walks,
barefoot in the soft soil
turned by her uncovering.
She walks alone
but leaves a path that others
might find their way.
And no one comes to listen,
but she speaks out loud,
lungs full with the breath
of the whispering trees
calling down the wind,
"I'm coming,
I'm coming."
And her uncertain
faithful steps
could lead us into life.

Working order

I move my arms
like a crane operator
moves the machinery,
with an automatic shift.
I sit inside
the cab of my head
that I thought
was the heart of the matter,
and work the gears
that lift and drop
and dig into the earth,
but I never feel
how the claw or the clay
feels.
No dirt beneath
my fingernails,
no notice of cool or warmth.
There is a nerve,
an electrical circuit
that runs from here to there,
but not from there to here,
it works one way.
I've cut the wires
and they need to be spliced,
replaced to working order,
so I can touch the stones
that I use to build my life.

ASK WHY

Since 1903
the walls in this house
have held
the ceiling up.
Long cracks
of plaster and paper
fold into full veins
running the length
to the floor,
carrying life
back
to the hearth.
Ghostly gardens
that once grew greens
gave food
to the families
and work
to the women.
I can still feel
their memories here,
singing
low in the silence,
grounding us all lightly
and safely
while we sleep.
Babies lived here.
Babies that grew
into men
and then
grew old and died,
leaving nothing
but a hollow space
in the walls.

Neighbor ladies
sat on steps
in the evening
of summer, listening
to push mowers
and children laughing
at the end of day
which came
so late at night.
They had hair nets on
and print cotton dresses,
aprons over top,
and their hair
grew gray
under incandescent light
while cooking
the evening meal.
I can see
the women here,
feel them
in my breath,
but the men
were always absent
from their homes.
On their way
to their graves,
perhaps,
without thinking
to stop
and ask why.

HISTORY

I can feel
the history in the making
resting here
in the evening shade
of generations that passed
like a flash of lightning
in the wrinkled blinking
of elderly eyes.
Time eases into spaces,
settles and sets
and records its
sweet slow music
in the groove of our days.
My pen becomes the needle
to play it back
before it's gone,
lost in the sweeping up
of our debris.
My children's children
saw through me today
in a layer of time
unfolding.
Unmade eyes
great with interest
as their fathers bathed
together, both of them
easily fitting in one bath.
This is the place
where I grew up,
they said, in the echoes
of my future.
These are the opening spaces
of time yet to be.

TRAINS OF THOUGHT

What goes on
in your little boy brain
with synapses snapping
like hot wires
welding tiny tracks
into place,
do they transport
your timeless trains
of thought?
Sleeper trains
that travel all night
go non-stop
to your destinations
while you rock and bump
in your bunk
and miles of mindless prairie
pass in purple silence.

GOD ANSWERS

What do you ask me
that you do not already know?
Where do you think I am
that you are not
in that same place always?
When you rise up,
am I not in the tender lifting
of your arms?
How can I know all things
until you remember
who you are?
Why ask questions
when you are the answer
of all answers?

BE A WILD FIELD

Be a wild field
of grass and weeds,
growing as tall
as you can
in places
and lying down
in others.
The drunken lover
could lay in that grass
and be holy
in your arms.
Be the dandelion who
doesn't compare herself
to the rose
in the bucket
at the florists shop.
Let yourself
open full to the sun
and close
to the cold of night.
Be the tree
that stands in that field
smiling
in his sleep.
Don't look
for the gardener's
clearing shears
to cut back
the lengths
you'll go to.

CYCLE

How can I resist my nature?
The moon draws me in
and lets me out
like a mother
rocking her baby to sleep
and I resist the dark.
I dig in my heels
as if refusing
could stop
the turning of time.
The earth evolves
and women age,
while men
just grow grey
at the temples.
The ebb and flow
of waves on my sea
will end on a distant shore,
and I can flow on the top
or get cramps on the bottom.

Triangle

Everything turns to sexual seeking
as I notice the wedge between my mind
and understanding. One true triangle
in the noticeable shapes of nature.
Two small circles to round it out,
all the rest, the same as any man's.
The length of hair and fingernails,
the whisper of a whisker,
throw on a coat of paint
and you'll look just fine.
Indoor/outdoor plumbing,
all the same to some.
Except the right to bear arms
and fruit
and burdens
divided differently.
If my stomach is rounder than my breast,
will they name me again to live in a pen?
But I do live in a pen, if you get my point.
I got yours, and look where it got me.
Saddle bags where I carry the things
that I can't leave home without.
Torn tender tissue,
memories and mammories
full then flat, flapping in the breeze.
Scars of stretching myself too thin
to carry your load, and mine.
I was a little bit of a chicken
in the egg of life,
but now I'm a mother hen,
trying to let go and let god,
and the woman,
grow life inside of me.

GO TO POT

I slice the hair
from beneath my arms,
I clip and pluck,
polish and paint,
get lost in a cloud of powder
as I puff in the buff
on the bathroom floor.
I scrub and style
myself into shape
to make the most
of womanly means,
but where are written the rules
of what womanly means?

Who said that hair
shouldn't grow down there,
that legs should be bare
or that I should care?
I lavish with loads of lotion
so I'm smooth to the touch
of some man's hands,
but dare not take any pleasure
in putting it on.

Why is it I think
of what *they'll* think
as I suck in the curve
so my zipper won't swerve
and slip off the right track
so I can't get back
in the jeans
that are the means
to my end?

The products are spilling
all over the floors,
from out of the drawers
and behind the doors
that I'm sure
could keep me
in fantastic feminine form.

Well maybe Miss Scarlet
was a cinch to cinch
to a 13 inch
with very little pinch
but my thighs
are already that size
so there's really no hope.

Our mothers would
hurdle in girdles
to get to the side
of secretarial pools
where they would lounge
on the deck of the desk
with their legs
in a tangle,
trying to catch the eye
of any bachelor
passing by,
or anything else
they could catch
with the flash of a lash.

But because they could
barely breathe, their brains

must've been
severely damaged,
to pass this bill of goods
down to us as we bloomed.
(Oh and hot house flowers
don't smell as sweet,
so we'll need to use
perfumes.)

And what if I didn't
spend so much time
in the toilet
watering myself?
They'd surely say,
"Oh she's really let herself
go to pot!"

JANITOR IN A DRUM

Why do women always get the job
of cleaning the bathroom bowl?
Sharing equal work and pay
and doing dishes and dens and diapers,
I wonder why men will never
touch a toilet.
Not that I'm naming names, of course,
but I'm not the one who misses.
My aim is better than his
and he can point!
Commercials never show Big John
in a john with a brush in his hand,
or standing on his head
to get under the rim.
I've mastered this task
and it's time to move on
to new and greater heights,
cleaning the gutters
might be a fair exchange.
And perhaps he can start
with the shower stall
and work his way down to his knees
to pray for a savior, a saint,
or a janitor in a drum.

Busses

Busses are like men.
There's one along
often enough
and I know I'll
pay the price
for my ride
with some small token
of appreciation.
Some take many
women up town
who'd have no other way
to get there.
But you can get on
and off
whenever you like,
take the passes
and pass them along
to the next one
down the pike.
They have access to
the fast lane,
but are generally
running behind,
and they carry
a lot of stuff around
but they're slow,
and I don't know
how to fix them.

TAKE YOUR TIME

I don't want your tongue
shoved down my throat,
a probe, a plunger,
hungry enough
to see what I had
for dinner.
And I don't want some
syrupy, slobery suck
stuck to me like
a suction cup.
If you come in here
you watch your step
and mind
your P's and Q's,
and choose your words
quite carefully,
don't mumble
as you
mouth them to me.
I read lips,
you know,
and yours are scared
and starved and tired
and try to perform some
one act
streetcar named desire.
But the fire I want
is in your mind
and slightest hesitation,
and your destination
will come
if you only
take your time.

Unwanted Attention

Just a little sexy,
but not enough
to deserve being raped.
Pretty,
but not like I know it
or flaunt it around.
Men's eyes
move over me,
my face, my neck,
down and back
and through
the mist of mystery
like a dream
they thought they'd had.
If I made myself
ugly or fat
they'd stay away,
but so would I.
I'd leave myself
in a trailer
somewhere
eating pig's feet and
reading romance novels
to feel what I felt
when I wanted
unwanted attention.

SWALLOWED THE KEY

I'd love to get lost
in the blue of your eyes,
come in for a swim,
but there is no lifeguard
there.
I could rest
in the mountains
of your shoulders,
lay loose in the roots
of your legs,
breathe deep
in the clearing
of your soul,
but I'd be alone.
You're absent
from the call,
your body numb
and hypnotized
glides
through the day
while you're locked away.
You knock,
but I can't come in.
You ache,
but I can't make you open.
You can see
through the hole
where I stand,
but you've
swallowed the key.

SPENT

Sometimes the lovemaking
is better than the orgasm.
Long lingerings at almost
leave you here inside of me,
lost and lazy and tired
of fighting waves
of what will come and pass
like a slow train
while you're waiting
at the tracks.

A fast finish flashes
a light in the night
but leaves you blind,
unable to see what lays
before your eyes
and out of time
and energy, spent like
a 49¢ impulse item
that you wanted
but really don't care
if it lasts or not.

The time it takes
to slide inside me
through your eyes
is time spent like
a treasured silver dollar
that your father
gave you as a boy.
You slip it into the slot
of the machine
where life's a gamble,

---

but you pull and release
slowly, keeping your hand
steady on the handle,
and you see the matches
made across your eyes
reflecting mine
in the glass face
you're staring into,
and you see you've won.

Come invest another,
take a chance.
You may make out
like a bandit,
or maybe just spend
a little time
and get nothing in return
but a little exercise
for your arm
while wrestling
with the truth
that the game only works
real well
when you've nothing
to lose.

PERIOD

The menopausal woman pauses
to put a period
at the end of the period
of her period.
Now she waxes
primarily at the parlor
and wanes
in a permanent wave,
the tide going out to sea
as she stands on the shore.
She keeps abreast of her breasts
and the size of her thighs
and the crinkle of wrinkles,
and curls the pearls around
her ringless fingers.
She cools the hots
and warms cold nights
in a flash
with a handful of hormones
and diet pills washed down
with a cup of caffeine.
Then verve and vivarin
and no-doz to keep her
from nodding in her module
at the job where she spent
twenty years
on useless dues.
Then home to a silent house
where sominex, sleep-eze
and nytol wait
to kiss her to sleep
and hold her
through moonless nights.

Come to Your Senses

In a sense
I see you smiling,
sorrow sadly
mistaken for joy.

In a sense
I feel you reaching,
longing to touch
what you only destroy.

In a sense
the smell surrounds you,
the taste of death
lies warm on your tongue.

I hear you cry
from across the miles,
but you're deaf
to your own
lost innocence.

Cutting room floor

Words
from scenes
that play back in my mind,
voices
that haven't
spoken in years
still hiss in static feedback
from the tape recorder inside.
The background noise
destroys my thoughts,
I have to cut it out
before it performs
some monologue
in the drama
of my children's lives.

People in hell want ice water.
Don't speak until you're spoken to.
Sit down, straighten up,
don't you talk back to me.
Just who do you think you are?

Children were meant to be seen
and not heard.
Because I said so, that's why.
You make me sick.
You think you're so smart.
How could you be so dumb?

Act your age.
Oh just grow up.
Don't ask such stupid questions.

Leave me alone,
get out of my sight.
You do as you're told right now.

Sit up, speak up, shut up,
I'm talking to you,
answer me when I speak!
What's the matter, you deaf?
Don't you sass me like that.
Now that's it, I have spoken.

If you don't sit still
I'll hit you so hard
it'll make your head spin,
or blister your ass so black and blue
that you won't sit down for a week.

I'll give you someting to cry about,
so just shut your trap and get off my back.
You're really askin for it, this time
you've really made me mad.

Don't make me hit you,
I'm warning you.
Not another word, now
I'm through talking!

Good.
Because I'm through listening,
too.

TIRED

I'm tired.
Too tired to work
and worry, hurry
and bury myself.
I don't do
a day's doing,
heavy with
heaving and healing.
Vacantly listening,
listless and lazy,
crazy to cry out loud.
Lost lonely longings
slow sorrow seeping,
psychology sewing it up.
Guilty galavanting,
choked chuckling,
energy spent
and then exchanged
for something else,
something
a little more me.

APATHY

Compressing
in from the edges,
the outer layers
harden and numb.
Inside,
now by myself,
the screams are fading
down hollow hallways
in wings
I've closed off
for the winter.
Cold grows into stone
like something living,
the warmth of life escapes
like something
letting in it's death
like a thief,
resigned and lying down.
I struggle
against my apathy
and lose,
hands down.
So I'll sleep through the season
and wait
for the spring
again.

Consumption

You sit in a booth
in the drive in diner
of my dream,
half lidded self righteousness
staring sideways.
All the family is there
sharing a meal with you
where I was uninvited,
but showed up unexpectedly,
like I always do,
not knowing why,
like a fly
drawn to dung
in a field full of flowers.
I stand at the counter
waiting for service,
but instead,
I get the business.
Stuck between my needs
and your impressions
I wait, half frozen
smile on my face
of the corpse
I almost became.
But instead the ammonia of you
pours into the soda of me
and I press and pound
to the surface,
"Would you please
get over here
and take my order?"
He sneers and staggers
in his own sweet time

to torture my grasp for power.
You sit
with shaking head
and rolling eyes
and deem disgusted judgement,
"When will that girl
ever learn some manners."
I won't roll over onto
the stainless steel counter
of your red meat morgue
to be laid out
and dressed for death
with false color on my cheeks
and lipstick painting
my mouth into a shut smile
leaving a nice, last impression.
I came here
for food for thought
and nourishment for my soul.
I'll pound my fist on the
counter of your consumption
and pay my tab
for whatever I owe,
but I won't stand
stupidly silent for you.

DON'T LOOK BACK

with thanks to John Bradshaw

Don't look back
you'll turn to stone,
petrify in the presence
of the truth
of the lies.
Pretend not to know
what you saw
as you go, lose it
in the desert of your mind.
Or be the salt of the earth,
a pillar of your
community
while the smart ones
run like hell.
Sodom and Gomorrah
were just your
old home towns,
it's best
to try to forget.
Turn the other cheek,
but not all the way around
or you'll be standing
as your own tombstone.
Take the fear of God
and fear for your lives
should you ever try
to recover yourself
from the sand
that time sent storming
across your tracks.
Remember,
whatever you do,
just don't look back.

PRISONERS

for Alice Miller

We keep them
prisoners of childhood,
bound to fail
in double bind rules.
In a three legged race
we tie them to a tree,
struggling
to rip up the roots
and move forward.
The judges and wardens
warn against weaning them
from our covert captivity.
Keep them calm,
control their concerns,
drug them with
psychedelic animation
and keep them very,
very quiet. Fill
their heads with
parts of speech that
never fit together
into coherent sentences,
where they might
understand their rights
or appeal
our convictions.

SHELTER

I scoop up my truth
like stew at the shelter.
Nothing fancy,
a clean spoon
for a dirty mouth.
You may not like
to look inside
at the soiled and sore
and starving,
occasionally offensive
and often awful,
but I've nowhere
left to go.
I don't want to bother
with brotherly lies,
so I'll sit here
in the doorway.
Can't go in,
I don't have a key
or a clue
where the next meal's
coming from.

IN THE SHADE

I seduce death
while secretly
longing for life.
Sultry stares
into the inevitability
of sleeping in the shade
of death's embrace
laid close against
my quiet breast,
taken,
in the end,
with no will left,
I snap sharply at life
as it reaches
a hand to hold me
till I go.

Cocaine

Cocaine came like a lover
to an inexperienced girl
on a cold night.
New and strong,
taking charge
of my clumsy naivete'.
It held me shaking
with icy hands,
stared long
in my mirrored eyes,
drank my breath,
pulsed with my heart
in sultry, excited poundings.
It danced me over the edge
of cracking ice and fear of life,
into smooth sheets
and satin smiles
in the shadow
of melting mouths.
I was loved
like no other
had ever loved me.
I flew to new heights
of confidence,
defined my womanly wants.
Stood straight and tall
like a model of ingenuity.
I numbed my teeth
to take greater bites of life
with insatiable hunger,
but forgot
the food for thought
left stale on my plate.

I became brilliant
with razor sharp wit,
cut
with cutting edge humor.
I laughed
all the way to the bank
till I saw
the coupling
had started to cost me.
Like a prostitute
you thought had loved you,
it left
and took its toll.
My weight in golden days
that turned to brass
and hardened like metal,
my sunken treasured eyes
in sleepless nights.
I saw myself in the mirror
starting to die
one line at a time,
the wreckless wrinkles
of time
that's spent too fast,
and left myself
alone again
at last.

Barbara

Her voice has the constancy
of mothering.
I've never heard it,
but I can feel it
in my muscles, relaxing,
like darvon in the hospital
where someone cares for you
all the time.
Clean white sheets
surround me, and I don't
have to think about anyone,
not even myself.
Just let the brain
go numb with the limbs
and drink in breath
like liquid quenching
all the cells of my body.
Pour me out my pores
and let me leak along the floor,
where someone else
can wipe up the spill
and wring me into the sink,
where I will drain back
into the source
of all liquid
and all life
where I belong,
safe inside the circle.
Any point in a thousand,
melding together
where separation is meaningless
in the one well
of wellness.

MINDLESS SPIRIT

I would have you.
Come to my breast
and breathe
your long silence
into mine.
Don't make words
out of right angle thoughts
when you're near me.
My mindless spirit
already lays open
to meet
and mingle with yours.
If we could take time
out of its circle
and feel it's hands
dance rhythms
around us
too soothing and slow
to keep us wound tight,
you'd be here
with me
tonight.

Unfinished Business

I dream unfinished business.
Long reaching out through layers of time
to settle the dust of my past.
Haunting hours of hollow holding,
words that went without saying,
I never knew I needed to see you
again.

I draw you into the drawing room
of destinies undone
where I change the course
of the outcomes, pull back
all things I've lost,
utter truths never listened to
and loosen the knot in my stomach.

Then disappear the dream
into caves of dark past hollow places,
where they haunt like ethers,
invisible and pungent
as if I had just been there.
Smelling you, drinking you in
in full swallows of breath,
I'm satisfied at the flavor,
the taste you left in my mouth.

MIRRORS

I am no one's enemy,
I can be no one's judge.
I am not the problem,
or the solution you seek
to soothe your soul.
I am not the star performer,
rather an audience to myself.
I am here on the stage
of my own curtain rising
and play
for my own amusement.
But you can watch.
Of course,
it's all done with mirrors.

ACTION

Marjorie Moodswing,
Kiss me Kate,
Fuck you Frank and
They'll Never Get Me Again Greta,
all characters developed for the play.

The piece in the game
where the rules changed daily,
hourly, like viruses mutating
to stay alive once a cure
had been invented.

Perfect Penny
or Vicious Viktor,
Shrinking Violet,
Manipulative Marge,
never quite disintegrated
pre-integrated schiz.

The roles were written for me
by my forefathers
(and two mothers).
I stepped in, script in hand,
and the rest of my body
through genetics,
sunk so deep into my cells
I thought it was me.

And like an actress who thinks
the camera could always be on,
I performed perfectly.
Even in the shower
or alone, asleep in my bed.

And like a pro,
I'd cheat out
toward my best side
whenever I could.

Cut, curtain, call it a wrap.
Bad reviews
kept audiences away.
The run is over, long as it was,
but the characters got stale,
and actors show-and-tell'ish
in their performances.

The sets have faded like
wallpaper flowers and fallen
in the dust and debris
as the bad guys died in the dirt
of the demolished stage.

Time for Casual Cathy
to close the book
before there's another scene.
So slip inside
the shammy soft jeans,
push up the sleeves
and check the mascara,
place bag and coat comfortably
over one shoulder.
Then tousle the hair
for that windswept look
and drift on out the door.

And, action.

THIS IS GROWING OLD

I have seen myself at sixty
shaking a scarred and crooked finger
at someone else's fault.
Back stiff from foolish fencing,
staying straight and taut on my toes
when I could have been dancing
instead.
Face tensed into a frown of folds
where there could have been
lines of laughter.
Tongue cracked from lashing out hard
at the whipping boy of the hour,
instead of loose and relaxed
like long longing that's been loved.
My head a brittle bun
of splitting hairs,
eyes that pierce like pins when
they could have plunged like pools.
They say you can't change the future,
but today I'll take a step
and clear a clean new path
on which to place myself
and pace myself
to grow graceful
as I go.

GOODBYE

to my father

Without closure,
I still feel a slight draft of warm air
escape through the crack
in the door of my heart,
I'm smart, but I don't know
how to reach the knob from here.
There's a stop in the way,
something unsaid
that's caught in my throat
like a creaking hinge that cries,
but has no words to speak its sorrow.
What caused us to come together,
what to come apart?
And why did you never
close the door completely?
Your hand never touched the knob,
the wind from your leaving
blew it almost all the way back
to where it had been
before I opened and let you in.
I didn't even see you slip out
you left without any words,
and I hadn't any I trusted yet
to tell you how I missed you.
You don't arrive
you never leave,
you aren't here
and I can't get you out
of my mind,
all this time,
all I wanted to say
was goodbye.

Afterlife death dream

Could it be
you've been waiting for me
to kill you
all this time?
One final
act of love
to free you
from my existence?
Thirty three years
I've dragged you around,
pounds of weight
to make my journey
slow and arduous,
could it have been
because you
were unwilling to go?
Thursday morning
I took your life,
sliced it from mine
with your hunting knife,
saw myself stab into
your long dead body.
No blood came out,
I saw inside, your soul
had long since
left it's shell
and you celebrated
release
from the hell
where you've waited
since the day you died,
waited to be let go
so you could rise.

Coming Light

I'm passing through
the light bearing years
and seeking solace
in the shadows,
the shallow dark
that seeps
before the deep.
The outside cleansed
I walk within
to see the soil
of my uncovering.
Standing tall
I linger
at the forest's edge
at night,
the dawn of dusk's
still light
my final sight
of sorrow passing.
An earthly calm
replaces it
easy as moon
takes over
for sun,
and shows the truth
in the darkest
coming light.

FULL CIRCLE

I am two dimensional words
longing for depth.
All around me
the roundness of life,
and I speak one straight line
to you.
I want to open
into the circle,
root my feet and fly
my arms in the air
and pull it inside.
But what can breathe in life?
What can cause
continual wholeness?
If I find that river
I will drink it till I'm full
and my thirst is quenched.
But what invocation will bring it?
How can we all live our lives
at once
inside my body?
I want to feel your breathing
inside my chest.
I want to praise like a poet,
grieve like a Christ,
to see the end of my actions
as if they were the beginning,
coming around
full circle,
back to meet me ❦

Vicky Edmonds is available for speaking engagements,
readings of her work and writing classes
for children, teenagers and adults.

Please look for her upcoming books,

once drunk...
(of learning to be with and without men)

&

opening
(the next possibility)

Also look for her books on tape,
cards, calendars and posters.

Broadsides of individual poems
are available as well.

For more information or to order this book
or other writings by Vicky Edmonds,
please call or write to:

e) all of the above

4742 • 42nd Avenue SW, Suite 607, Seattle, WA 98116
(206) 937-0700 • (206) 763-6702
fax (206) 763-7627